CONTENTS

Words in **bold** are in the glossary.

Rolling with technology

A racing car speeds across the finish line. A giant dumper truck carries a huge load of rocks. Its tyres are twice the height of an average man. These vehicles are very different, but they are both cool rides on wheels!

Giant dumper trucks can carry heavy loads of rocks, soil and other materials.

COOL RIDES ON WHEELS

ELECTRIC RACING CARS, SUPERBIKES AND MORE

by Tammy Gagne

Raintree is an imprint of Capstone Global Library Limited, a company incorporated in England and Wales having its registered office at 264 Banbury Road, Oxford, OX2 7DY – Registered company number: 6695582

www.raintree.co.uk
myorders@raintree.co.uk

Edited by Carrie Sheely
Designed by Juliette Peters
Original illustrations © Capstone Global Library Limited 2022
Picture research by Jo Miller
Production by Katy LaVigne
Originated by Capstone Global Library Ltd
Printed and bound in India

978 1 3982 0348 8 (hardback)
978 1 3982 0347 1 (paperback)

British Library Cataloguing in Publication Data
A full catalogue record for this book is available from the British Library.

Acknowledgements
We would like to thank the following for permission to reproduce photographs: Alamy: JuistLand, 21; Getty Images: Frederic J. Brown, 11, Gerlach Delissen - Corbis/Contributor, 26, picture alliance/Contributor, 15; Newscom: Kyodo, 7, Reuters/Ivan Alvarado, 25, ZUMA Press/Barry Sweet, 10, ZUMA Press/Ben Birchall, 23 (Bottom); Shutterstock: 1000 Words, 27, Action Sports Photography, 9, betto rodrigues, 16, HQuality, 29, Kuznetsov Alexey, Cover, Mariusz Niedzwiedzki, 6, Mark_studio, 5, mimmikhail, 19, Monthong, 17, Oskar SCHULER, 14, Piotr Zajac, 8, Popsuievych, 4, Suwin, 28; U.S. Air Force photo by Staff Sgt. Christopher Hubenthal, 23 (Top); Wikimedia/Iannismardell, 12, 13. **Design elements:** Capstone; Shutterstock: teerayut tae.

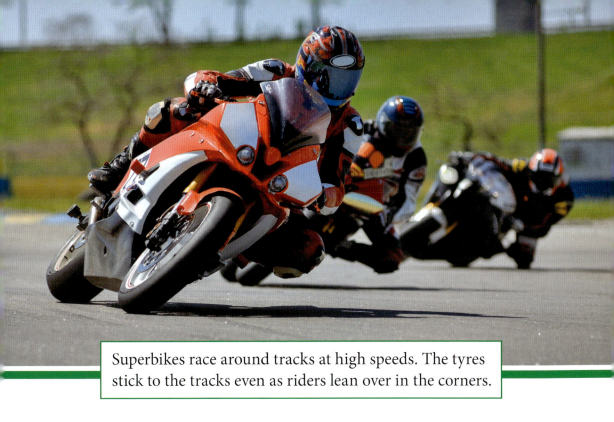

Superbikes race around tracks at high speeds. The tyres stick to the tracks even as riders lean over in the corners.

Wheeled vehicles come in many forms. Supercars such as the McLaren 720S can reach very high speeds. Other vehicles on wheels can travel **off-road** as easily as they can on streets. Some have many wheels while others have just one or two.

Modern **technology** has made wheeled vehicles more advanced than ever before. Some vehicles are self-driving. Others have high-tech **sensors** for top performance. Let's see what awesome vehicles are rolling around!

ATVs

All-**terrain** vehicles (ATVs) are perfect for adventure in the great outdoors. Mud, snow and sand are no problem for these tough vehicles. They can speed right through! Some people use ATVs as transport in **rural** areas. Other people ride them just for fun.

ATVs are built to go off-road. The tyres have a series of bumps and grooves called tread. They provide good grip on dirt and other loose surfaces. ATVs also have narrow bodies to fit into small spaces. Their tough **suspension systems** can handle big bumps and jumps.

Strong suspension systems allow ATV riders to take huge jumps without rough landings.

For some riders, speed and power are important. ATV racers want to beat others to the finish line. Emergency workers might need to make rescues on ATVs. The fastest ATVs can travel at more than 121 kilometres (75 miles) per hour.

Autonomous Work Vehicle

Honda is testing its Autonomous Work Vehicle. This self-driving ATV does not need a person on it to control it. Instead, it uses sensors and other systems as it travels. This ATV has helped workers perform various jobs. It has carried supplies for firefighters up steep hills. It has also towed a mower to cut down weeds in tight spaces.

Monster trucks

A monster truck speeds around a turn. It almost tips, but it keeps going! It sails over a jump and lands with a thud. The crowd goes wild! Monster trucks are some of the coolest machines on four wheels. At shows, monster trucks race and do amazing stunts. They jump over big lines of cars. Some can jump more than 9 metres (30 feet) in the air. They also spin in fast circles and do giant wheelies.

A driver in the Monster Jam series performs at a show in Poland.

In freestyle events in the Monster Jam series, drivers are judged on their stunts.

Their large size sets monster trucks apart from ordinary pick-up trucks. Many monster trucks are 3.7 m (12 feet) tall. Many monster truck tyres are 1.7 m (5.5 feet) tall and 1 m (3.5 feet) wide. The tyres can weigh between 363 and 408 kilograms (800 and 900 pounds).

Monster trucks get banged around in shows. Their bodies and many other parts must be repaired or replaced often.

Arcimoto FUV

The Arcimoto FUV looks a bit like a go-kart on three wheels. But unlike most go-karts, it is for driving on streets. FUV stands for "Fun Utility Vehicle". It can carry the driver and one passenger. Like a motorbike, the FUV has handlebars instead of a steering wheel. The vehicle's side doors can come off. Heated seats add comfort on cooler days.

The FUV is an electric vehicle. Its electric motor uses power from a battery. It can drive about 161 km (100 miles) before the battery needs to be recharged. The FUV can reach a top speed of 121 km (75 miles) per hour.

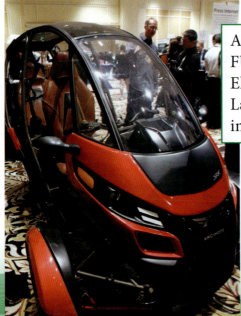

Arcimoto showed off its FUV at the Consumer Electronics Show in Las Vegas, Nevada, USA, in 2016.

The driver and passenger wear seat belts in an FUV.

Different types of FUV

Arcimoto wants to offer more types of FUVs. The company thinks the vehicle would be a great delivery vehicle. It could help companies get food and small packages to their customers. Arcimoto also might equip the vehicle to be used for medical emergencies and firefighting. The company began testing this Rapid Responder version in 2019.

Zarooq SandRacer 500 GT

Most vehicles are made for either street or off-road riding. But the Zarooq SandRacer 500 GT performs great on both. This sports car has a top speed of 221 km (137 miles) per hour. Many of the fastest sports cars can reach more than 402 km (250 miles) per hour. But unlike these faster cars, the SandRacer can keep going past the end of the road.

The SandRacer was built to look like rally cars. These cars race long distances off-road.

Bumpy tyres allow the SandRacer to grip off-road surfaces.

The SandRacer has a body made completely out of carbon fibre. This material makes it both lightweight and strong. The SandRacer weighs 1,300 kg (2,866 pounds). The average mid-size steel car weighs about 1,495 kg (3,300 pounds).

Drivers can adjust the SandRacer's height. They can make it sit higher for off-road use. This helps keep it from getting stuck in mud or other tough off-road conditions.

Formula E cars

Formula 1 (F1) and Formula E cars look a lot alike. But F1 cars are petrol powered. Electricity powers Formula E cars. These exciting electric vehicles arrived on the racing scene in 2014.

Porsche, BMW and Mercedes Benz all compete in Formula E racing. A team can choose its own **drivetrain**. This system of parts delivers power to the wheels. Each car also has unique computer **software**. Teams use it to try to get an edge over their competitors.

Formula E car driver Oliver Turvey practises for a race in Berne, Switzerland.

Formula E cars cannot yet move as fast as F1 cars. But they can still reach impressive speeds. The cars have a top speed of about 280 km (174 miles) per hour. They can also reach 100 km (62 miles) per hour in 2.8 seconds.

a Formula E race in Berlin, Germany

 FACT

Many F1 races are at permanent tracks. Each Formula E track is unique. Races are often held in the middle of big cities.

Superbikes

Superbikes are some of the fastest rides on two wheels. Riders push these bikes to their limits in the Superbike World Championship and other racing series.

Superbikes have large engines that are built for speed. Motorcycle engine size is measured in ccs, or cubic centimetres. A superbike's engine size is usually between 800 and 1,200 ccs.

The Kawasaki Ninja H2R is among the fastest superbikes. It has a top speed of 401 km (249 miles) per hour. The motorbike is built just for racing. The H2R's engine has a specially built supercharger. This part draws more air into the engine to boost power. The H2R's body design helps the bike cut through the air. It helps the bike go faster.

The Kawasaki Ninja H2R has a lightweight carbon fibre body.

Racers speed around the track in a Superbike World Championship race in Thailand.

The Lightning LS-218 is the world's fastest electric superbike. It can go 351 km (218 miles) per hour. It can last 241 km (150 miles) between battery charges.

 FACT
The Kawasaki Ninja H2R has special paint. It can repair small scratches by itself!

Fat tyre bikes

Fat tyre bikes go places that other bicycles can't. They can move through sand. They can even ride through snow.

People who ride fat tyre bikes can ride them in any sort of weather. The extra-wide tyres are designed not to crack. Even icy corners are no match for them.

Many fat tyre bikes have just one speed. This means that riders have to work harder in some places. Riding a fat tyre bike can give people a great workout!

Riders can make the tyres fatter or thinner by changing the **tyre pressure**. The fatter the tyres are, the more comfortable the ride is. Fatter tyres also grip the ground better.

Knobbly tyres on fat tyre bikes
help grip snowy and icy surfaces.

From mountain bike to fat tyre bike

Not everyone needs to buy a special bike model to have a fat tyre bike. Riders can add fat tyres to some mountain bike frames. Riders simply swap their original tyres for the fatter ones. They can then change back to mountain bike tyres for everyday use. Ordinary tyres are usually better for dry and solid ground.

M35 cargo truck

The M35 cargo truck has been getting big jobs done for 70 years. It can carry loads that weigh 2.5 tonnes. For this reason, people sometimes call the M35 the "Deuce and a Half". *Deuce* relates to the number two.

AM General and other companies built the M35 to replace some of the US military's trucks used in World War II (1939–1945). They started with the frame of a four-wheel-drive off-road truck.

The M35 carries large weapons and other heavy supplies. It moves troops from place to place. A trailer can attach to the back so it can carry even more.

Some M35s were designed with a flatbed to carry cargo.

One might think a truck so large would move slowly. But the M35 can drive up to 89 km (55 miles) per hour.

Unmanned ground vehicles

The US military needs information about enemies. But sending troops into enemy land can be dangerous. Instead, it can send unmanned ground vehicles (UGVs). UGVs are a cross between robots and vehicles.

The US Army and Marine Corps worked together to build the SARGE. The SARGE can safely travel onto the most dangerous battlefields. It has four cameras. They help the military watch enemy actions in the day or at night.

TerraMax technology allows regular military vehicles to become UGVs. The software takes over the vehicle's engine, steering and brakes. It can even program a vehicle to follow the vehicle in front of it.

A US Army soldier walks alongside a UGV being tested in Hawaii in 2016.

FACT

The Titan UGV has tracks like a tank's. It can carry 680 kg (1,500 pounds) of cargo.

Komatsu 930E dumper truck

Big jobs call for big trucks. The Komatsu 930E dumper truck is one of the biggest. It stands more than 7.3 m (24 feet) tall. The truck weighs more than 200 tonnes.

Mine workers use the Komatsu 930E truck. It can carry 320 tonnes of material. Mining dumper trucks must move uphill and downhill in steep areas. The truck remains steady even on the steepest hills. Its big engine provides plenty of power to make it up the hills. The 930E-4SE makes 3,500 horsepower. The average horsepower for a pick-up truck is about 275.

A Komatsu 930E's strong steel body helps it carry heavy loads.

FACT

The Komatsu 930E is so big that a driver must climb a ladder to reach the truck's cab.

McLaren 720S

Some people say the McLaren 720S supercar looks like a fighter jet. Others think it looks like a spaceship. But one thing is certain: it's built for speed!

What makes a supercar? There isn't an exact answer. But most are expensive cars designed to perform like racing cars. The McLaren 720S can blast from 0 to 97 km (60 miles) in 2.7 seconds. It has a top speed of 341 km (212 miles) per hour. Drivers can choose between three different driving modes.

A McLaren 720S was on display at the 2017 Geneva Motor Show in Switzerland.

The sleek body design of the McLaren 720S helps it cut through the air. This helps it reach high speeds.

One of the McLaren's coolest features is its doors. They don't open outwards. Instead, they open upwards. But their design isn't just for looks. As the car moves, air intakes in the doors push air to the car's **radiator**. This part keeps the engine from overheating.

The future of cool rides on wheels

The wheeled vehicles of the future will be even cooler than those of today. New technology will push supercars, racing cars and motorbikes to even faster speeds. Many car companies are working on building self-driving electric cars. They hope people will use these cars for everyday driving one day.

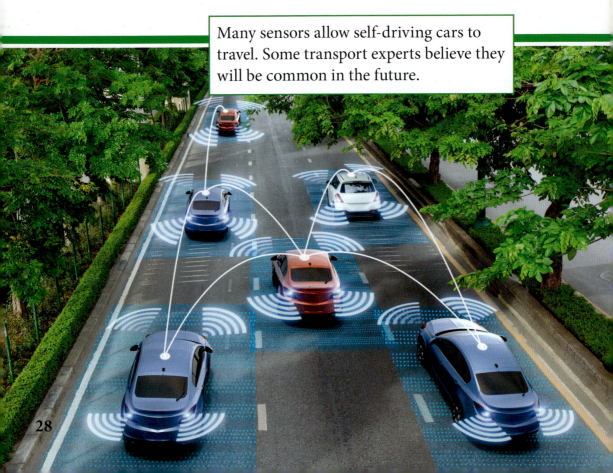

Many sensors allow self-driving cars to travel. Some transport experts believe they will be common in the future.

Designers work on a hologram for an electric car.

Toyota is working on a car with a special assistant. A **hologram** of a person will pop up from the dashboard whenever the driver needs help. It will give directions or explain the car's features.

No matter the type, wheeled vehicles of tomorrow are sure to be exciting. What would you like to drive?

GLOSSARY

drivetrain engine, gearbox and other parts that make a car move

hologram 3-D image formed by light

off-road designed to be driven on soil, mud, rock or other rough surfaces

radiator device through which a liquid circulates to cool a vehicle's engine

rural relating to an area in the country away from towns or cities

sensor instrument that detects changes and sends information to a controlling device

software programs that tell the hardware of the computer what to do

suspension system system of springs and shock absorbers that absorbs a vehicle's up-and-down movements

technology use of science to do practical things such as designing complex machines

terrain surface of the land

tyre pressure force that air inside a tyre has on its surface

FIND OUT MORE

BOOKS

Cars, Trains, Ships and Planes: A Visual Encyclopedia of Every Vechicle, DK (DK Children, 2015)

Great Car Designs 1900–Today (Iconic Designs), Richard Spilsbury (Raintree, 2016)

The History of Transport (The History of Technology), Chris Oxlade (Raintree, 2017)

Motion Projects to Build On (STEM Projects), Marne Ventura (Raintree, 2020)

WEBSITES

www.bbc.co.uk/bitesize/topics/zsxxsbk/articles/zxw6gdm
Learn about air resistance.

www.dkfindout.com/uk/transport/history-cars
Find out about the history of cars.

INDEX